STIR-FRY

Sunset Creative Cooking Library

By the Editors of Sunset Books

SUNSET BOOKS
President & Publisher: Susan J. Maruyama
Director, Finance & Business Affairs: Gary Loebner
**Director, Manufacturing
& Sales Service:** Lorinda Reichert

SUNSET PUBLISHING CORPORATION
Chairman: Robert L. Miller
President/Chief Executive Officer: Robin Wolaner
Chief Financial Officer: James E. Mitchell
Circulation Director: Robert I. Gursha
Editor, Sunset Magazine: William R. Marken

All the recipes in this book were developed and tested in the Sunset test kitchens. For information about any Sunset Book please call 1-800-634-3095.

The nutritional data provided for each recipe is for a single serving, based on the number of servings and the amount of each ingredient. If a range is given for the number of servings and/or the amount of an ingredient, the analysis is based on the average of the figures given. The nutritional analysis does not include optional ingredients or those for which no specific amount is stated. If an ingredient is listed with a substitution, the data was calculated using the first choice.

Nutritional analysis of recipes: Hill Nutrition Associates, Inc. of Florida.

Sunset Creative Cooking Library
was produced by St. Remy Press

Publisher: Kenneth Winchester
President: Pierre Léveillé
Managing Editor: Carolyn Jackson
Senior Editors: Elizabeth Cameron, Dianne Thomas
Managing Art Director: Diane Denoncourt
Administrator: Natalie Watanabe
Production Manager: Michelle Turbide
System Coordinator: Jean-Luc Roy
Proofreader: Garet Markvoort
Indexer: Christine Jacobs

COVER: *Shrimp & Vegetable Salad (page 61)*

PHOTOGRAPHY
*Victor Budnik: 6, 36, 42, 56; **Robert Chartier:** 14, 18, 23, 27, 41, 59; **Darrow M. Watt:** 4, 8, 9, 38, 48, 54; **Tom Wyatt:** 46, 52; **Nikolay Zurek:** 12, 16, 20, 24, 28, 30, 32, 34, 44, 50, 60, 62.*

PHOTO STYLING
*JoAnn Masaoka Van Atta: 36, 38, 44, 48, 54, 50, 56, 60, 62; **Lynne B. Morrall:** 42.*

ILLUSTRATIONS
Susan Jaekel: 11

ISBN 0-376-00901-2
Library of Congress Catalog Card Number 94-67313
Printed in the United States.

✇ printed on recycled paper.

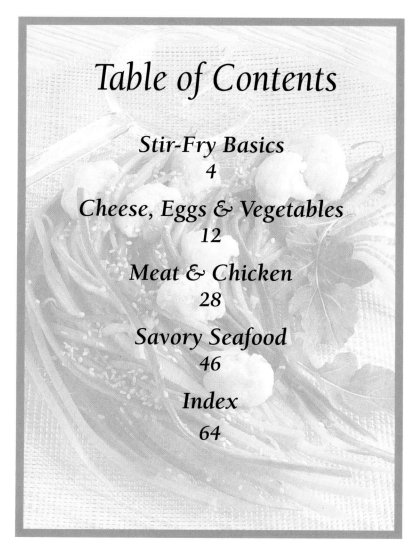

Table of Contents

S T I R - F R Y

Getting Started

When you think of wok cooking, you probably think immeditely of stir-frying—of quickly tossing and stirring bite-size pieces of meat and vegetables in a little hot oil, barely letting thcm touch the sides of the steep bowl. You likely picture Asian dishes, foods with crisp textures and the freshest of flavors. And stir-frying in a wok is, indeed, the one cooking method that is uniquely Asian—but it is surprisingly adaptable to many different foods.

Oriental stir-fries are by no means the only recipes a wok can handle. Though it may not be the universal utensil with as many uses as a Swiss army knife, this simple pan is undeniably versatile. It doubles as a deep-fryer; it's a perfect steamer for seafood, dumplings, pâtés, and even puddings. And stainless steel woks and those with a nonstick finish are ideal for stewing and braising.

Thanks to its unique shape, the wok is also a model of efficiency—the sloping sides and rounded bottom heat up quickly and evenly, and provide the greatest possible surface for cooking. Whether you use an electric or a gas range, you'll find that wok cookery saves you precious time and energy.

Choosing and caring for your wok

Woks are available in two basic shapes and a variety of sizes. The traditional wok has a rounded bottom, reflecting its original use—it was designed to be suspended in a brazier over a hot fire. The curved shape is as efficient as ever today, but the brazier has been replaced by a perforated ring stand that holds the wok steady on the range top.

A fairly recent introduction is the flat-bottomed wok, intended to sit directly atop burner or element. You'll need to purchase this style if you can't get a round-bottomed wok close enough to the heat source.

Woks typically have two handles, one on each side. Some models are equipped with wooden handle covers; if yours lacks this feature, you'll need to protect your hands with potholders when you cook. Woks that have a single long wooden handle also are available. They're easy to maneuver when you stir-fry—but when you want to lift a one-handled wok full of food or oil, be sure to lift it from both sides.

Woks range from 9 to 30 inches in diameter, but the 14-inch size is usually the best choice for home cooks; it's ample in capacity, yet simple to manage. Obviously, a wok of this size is also easier to store than a really big one would be—but all woks take up a fair amount of shelf space, and round-bottomed types tend to wobble instead of sitting flat. Many cooks find it is more convenient to hang woks from pot hooks than to keep them in a cupboard.

In addition to selecting the wok shape and size, you'll need to choose the best material for your needs. Woks were originally made of cast iron, but today the most commonly used metal is heavy-gauge rolled carbon steel. Carbon steel woks conduct heat well, making them great for stir-frying, but they do require seasoning and proper care to keep the surface in good condition and to prevent rusting.

Seasoning a carbon steel wok is a simple enough procedure. Before the first use, wash the wok with mild soapy water, then dry it directly over medium heat on your range until no moisture remains. Next, rub the inside with a paper towel dampened with about 2 teaspoons of salad oil. Wipe off any excess oil with a clean paper towel. After each use, wash the wok with sudsy water, using a dishwashing or bamboo brush to scrub out any food that has stuck to the surface. Then rinse well and dry again on the range. Keep in mind that, if not kept completely dry between uses, carbon steel woks will rust and will have to be cleaned and seasoned all over again before the next use.

Aluminum and stainless steel woks—often with copper bottoms and sides for improving heat conduction—are also available. These types need no seasoning; they won't rust, so you can simply clean them as you would any other alu-

In addition to using the right equipment, good Chinese cooking begins in the market. Adjust your menu or recipe to take advantage of the freshest vegetables available to you

minum or stainless pan. These woks are particularly good for steaming and stewing; they're fine for stir-frying, too, although they don't distribute heat as evenly as the carbon-steel woks do.

Most people agree that the top choice for tabletop cooking is the electric wok. They are especially suitable for poaching foods in hot broth, steaming, and deep-frying. But there is one disadvantage: because they tend to recover heat rather slowly after the food is added, they are not always successful for stir-frying.

Clean and care for your electric wok according to the manufacturer's directions, always removing the appliance's heat element before washing. If you've chosen a nonstick type model, use the proper utensils for stirring and for cleaning; sharp utensil will scratch the nonstick finish.

Four cooking sauces

Once you have made a recipe with the recommended sauce, try experimenting the next time using one of these four sauces.

Red Pepper Cooking Sauce
2 tsp. cornstarch
1/2 tsp. **each** crushed red pepper and salad oil
2 Tbsp. soy sauce
2 1/2 Tbsp. white wine vinegar
1/2 cup chicken broth or water

Oyster Cooking Sauce
1/2 cup water
1 Tbsp. dry sherry
2 Tbsp. oyster sauce or soy sauce

1/4 tsp. sugar
1 tsp. sesame oil
1 Tbsp. cornstarch

Chicken-flavored Cooking Sauce
1/3 cup chicken broth
1 Tbsp. soy sauce
1/2 tsp. sugar
1 Tbsp. oyster sauce (optional)

Coconut Milk Cooking Sauce
3/4 cup coconut milk (canned or thawed frozen)
3 Tbsp. **each** soy sauce, unseasoned rice
   vinegar or white wine vinegar
1 1/2 tablespoons fish sauce (*nam pla*) or
   soy sauce
1/2 to 1 tsp. crushed red pepper flakes

Stir-frying in a wok

When you stir-fry, you don't really fry; you cook foods quickly by stirring and tossing them in a small amount of hot fat. This kind of flash-cooking seals in juices and keeps flavors fresh; it's a technique you can use to make dishes of every kind, from appetizers to desserts. All stir-fry recipes follow the same basic steps; once you've mastered the method, you easily can create recipes of your own.

Stir-fried vegetables have bright color, crisp texture; chicken morsels are tender.

In addition to your wok, the only tool you need for successful stir-frying is a long-handled spatula with a wide, curved edge. Follow these steps for successful stir-frying:

1. Do all your cutting in advance. Foods should be cut into small, uniform pieces or thin slices (see pages 10-11.)

2. Prepare any seasonings and sauce mixtures in advance. Once you start to cook,

you won't have time to stop and create a sauce.

3. Assemble the cut-up meat and/or vegetables, seasonings, sauce mixture, and salad oil or other fat near the range.

4. Place a clean, dry wok over the heat specified in the recipe—typically high heat, sometimes medium or medium-high. When the wok is hot, add the fat as directed. Heat the oil until it's hot enough to ripple when the wok is tilted from side to side; if butter is called for, heat until it's foamy.

5. Add any seasonings (garlic, ginger, and crushed red pepper flakes, for example). Holding the wok handle in one hand and a wide spatula in the other, stir and toss the seasonings until they are lightly browned. Then add meat, if used. (Never add more than about 1 pound at a time; if you have

more, cook it in batches.) Spread the pieces evenly over the wok's surface; stir and toss until lightly browned all over. Turn meat out of wok.

6. Add 1 to 2 teaspoons more oil (or other fat). When the oil is hot, add vegetables, one variety at a time. Start with the type that has the longest cooking time; stir-fry just until tender-crisp to bite, lifting and tossing vegetables to coat them with oil. Turn the cooked vegetables out of the wok; repeat to cook remaining vegetables. (Or simply add all vegetables in sequence, timing your additions so all will be done at the same time.) For dense or fibrous vegeta-bles such as broccoli or asparagus, you may need to add a little water, then cover the wok and steam the vegetable slightly, stir-ring often.

7. Return meat and vegetables to the wok. Stir the cooking sauce to reblend corn-starch; then pour into wok. Stir until sauce boils and thickens. To serve the meal Chinese style, provide each diner with an individual bowl of steaming white rice.

NOTE: Use the cooking times given in our recipes as guides, not absolutes. Actual cooking time will vary, depending upon the kind of wok you use and the intensity of the heat source.

Cut foods in uniform pieces.

A wide spatula is an essential.

Cooking sauces thicken quickly.

Slicing and Chopping

Uniform cutting means uniform cooking. That's true no matter what method you use. But cutting pieces of equal size is particularly important for stir-frying recipes; because this cooking technique is so fast, there's no time for differences in ingredients' size and shape to even out. If you don't slice and chop evenly, the finished dish may well end up as a blend of undercooked, overdone, and just right.

Cutting into slanting or diagonal slices is a very effective way to cut through fibrous vegetables (celery, for example) and meat (such as flank steak) to tenderize them and to expose the greatest possible area to the sides of the heated wok.

The recipes in this book usually call for $1/8$- to $1/4$-inch-thick slanting slices. Make sure you use a very sharp knife or cleaver, and cut meat across the grain at a 45° angle. And here's a handy tip: you'll find that meat is much easier to slice uniformly when it's partially frozen.

Pay attention to a recipe's terminology. If ingredients are to be thinly sliced, it usually means cutting down rather than at a slant. Julienne strips should be about the size of a wooden matchstick. Diced foods should be cut into small cubes. Such consistent chopping and slicing contribute to both the preparation and presentation of any dish— one that tastes good and looks good, too.

Reducing sodium

If you frequently use your wok for Oriental-style cooking, you should think about the amount of sodium you may be consuming. Soy sauce, a basic seasoning in many of these recipes, can mean high levels of sodium. It's not too difficult to reduce the sodium content of most dishes, though.

You can use low-sodium soy sauce, season foods to taste with salt rather than adding the amount specified in the recipe, or simply cut down on serving sizes and round out the meal with plenty of plain rice or noodles. In China, rice is actually the bulk of the meal. A generous helping of steamed rice or boiled noodles serves another purpose, too—to soothe the palate when the main course is extra spicy.

To slice fibrous vegetables diagonally, cut them crosswise on the diagonal into $1/8$- to $1/4$-inch-thick slanting slices.

To slice meat, such as flank steak, cut uniformly across the grain at a 45° angle while the meat is partially frozen.

To slice such food as mushrooms thinly, cut straight down at a right angle.

To cut julienne strips, first cut into 2- to 3-inch lengths. Then cut into $1/8$-inch-thick slices, stack 2 or 3 at a time, and cut into $1/8$-inch-thick strips.

To dice food, such as potatoes, cut as directed for julienne strips, then cut crosswise into small squares. For larger dice, start with thicker strips.

Braising

For braising, follow the standard procedure of browning meat and briefly cooking vegetables in oil. Then add liquid, cover the pan, and simmer over low heat until ingredients are tender. To braise in a round-bottomed wok, you'll need a ring stand.

CHEESE, EGGS & VEGETABLES

Melted Cheese

*B*rie takes on an oriental flavor
when served as an appetizer with Crisp-fried Leaves
and Quail Eggs (pages 14 and 15).

∞

PER SERVING: *136 calories, 6 g protein, 10 g carbohydrates, 8 g total fat, 19 mg cholesterol, 238 mg sodium*

PREPARATION TIME: *10 min.*
COOKING TIME: *15 min.*

*1 small wheel (8 oz.) Brie
or Camembert cheese
1 baguette (8 oz.), thinly
sliced, toasted
2 cups Crisp-fried Leaves
(recipe on page 14)*

Place cheese in a 6- to 7-inch shallow pan or heat-proof dish. Bake, uncovered, in a 350° oven just until cheese begins to melt (12 to 15 minutes).

Set hot cheese on a tray. Place alongside in separate baskets or bowls the Crisp-fried Leaves and sliced and toasted baguette.

To eat, spread hot cheese on a toasted baguette slice and sprinkle with fried leaves.

Makes 12 appetizer servings

Crisp-fried Leaves

*F*ragile Crisp-fried Leaves make an intriguing garnish for
simple foods. You can make them ahead and store airtight at room
temperature in a paper-towel lined container for up to 3 days.

⌒

PER ¼ CUP: 32 calories, .20 g protein, .24 g carbohydrate, 3g total fat, 0 mg cholesterol, 6 mg sodium

PREPARATION TIME: *15 min.*
REFRIGERATION TIME: *1 hr.*
COOKING TIME: *10 min.*

*2 oz. leaves (spinach,
small-leaf mustard
greens, watercress, fresh
cilantro, flat-leaf or
curly parsley, or mint
Salad oil*

Remove and discard thick stems from leaves. Wash
leaves thoroughly, drain well, and pat dry. If you like,
cut across the grain into ¼-inch-wide strips. Wrap
leaves loosely in towels and enclose in a plastic bag.
Refrigerate for at least 1 hour to dry thoroughly.

Set a wok in a ring stand. Pour salad oil into wok
to a depth of about 2 inches and heat to 370°. Fry
greens a handful at a time (stand back; oil may splat-
ter). Turn leaves with a slotted spoon until they take
on a brighter green color and are at least partly
translucent (5 to 20 seconds); leaves may not turn
completely translucent in oil, but will become more
translucent as they stand. If leaves turn a darker
green and begin to scorch, they're overcooked.

Lift leaves from oil with a slotted spoon; drain on
paper towels. Serve hot or at room temperature.

Makes about 2 cups

Quail Eggs in Crisp-fried Nest

*Finger food at its best,
quail eggs add an exotic element to
your appetizer tray.*

∽

PER SERVING: *104 calories, 4 g protein, .91 g carbohydrate, 9 g total fat, 228 mg cholesterol, 9 mg sodium*

PREPARATION TIME: *15 min.*
COOKING TIME: *5 min.*

*12 to 18 quail eggs
1 Tbsp. sesame seeds
About 2 cups whole or
   shredded Crisp-fried
   Leaves (recipe opposite)
Salt*

Fill a 1- to 2-quart pan with about 2 inches of water; add eggs. Bring water to a boil; then reduce heat and simmer, uncovered, for 5 minutes. Drain and cover with cold water. Let stand until cool. Carefully shell eggs. (At this point, you may cover and refrigerate until next day.)

Toast sesame seeds in a small frying pan over medium heat until golden (about 2 minutes), shaking pan often. Set aside.

Pat eggs dry with a towel. Place Crisp-fried Leaves in a basket or bowl and nest eggs in leaves. Sprinkle sesame seeds and salt to taste over eggs and greens. Eat with fingers, picking up some of the greens with each egg.

Makes 4 to 6 appetizer servings

Zucchini Sticks

Elegantly garnished with enoki mushrooms and red bell pepper, a light side dish of briefly cooked Zucchini Sticks looks almost too good to eat.

∽

PER SERVING: 56 calories, 2 g protein, 5 g carbohydrates, 4 g total fat, 0 mg cholesterol, 5 mg sodium

PREPARATION TIME: *10 min.*
COOKING TIME: *4 min.*

*4 medium-size zucchini
 (about 1½ lb. total)
1 Tbsp. olive oil or salad oil
2 cloves garlic, minced
 or pressed
Pepper
Enoki mushrooms and red
 bell pepper (optional)
Grated Parmesan cheese
 (optional)*

Cut zucchini in half lengthwise. Then cut each half lengthwise into thirds.

Place a wok over medium heat; when wok is hot, add oil. When oil is hot, add zucchini and garlic and stir-fry gently until zucchini is tender-crisp to bite (about 3 minutes). Season to taste with pepper and serve immediately. If desired, garnish with mushrooms and bell pepper and offer grated cheese to sprinkle atop individual servings.

Makes 4 servings

Herb Eggs with Yogurt Sauce

*It's easy to make perfect scrambled eggs in your wok!
Here, the eggs are enlivened with fresh vegetables and served
with a minted yogurt sauce.*

PER SERVING: 252 calories, 15 g protein, 7 g carbohydrates, 18 g total fat, 440 mg cholesterol, 191 mg sodium

PREPARATION TIME: *15 min.*
COOKING TIME: *5 min.*

1 cup plain yogurt
*2 Tbsp. **each** minced green
  onion (including top)
  and fresh mint*
2 tsp. lemon juice
Dash hot pepper seasoning
8 eggs
2 Tbsp. water
1/4 tsp. pepper
1 Tbsp. butter or margarine
1 Tbsp. olive oil
1/2 cup minced parsley
*2 green onions (including
  tops), finely chopped*
*1 medium-size tomato,
  seeded, chopped*
Salt and pepper

Stir together yogurt, minced green onion and fresh mint, lemon juice, and hot pepper seasoning; set aside.

Beat eggs, water, and the 1/4 teaspoon pepper until blended.

Place a wok over medium heat; when wok is hot, add butter and oil. When butter is melted, add parsley and onions; stir-fry for 30 seconds. Add tomato and stir-fry for 30 seconds. Pour in eggs and stir gently until eggs are set but still moist (2 to 3 minutes). Season to taste with salt and pepper. Serve immediately with Yogurt Sauce.

Makes 4 servings

Szechwan Eggplant

Braised in broth that's richly flavored with pork and chiles, eggplant turns out savory and tender. Use either regular eggplant or the smaller, slimmer Japanese variety.

∽

PER SERVING: 293 calories, 7 g protein, 13 g carbohydrates, 25 g total fat, 20 mg cholesterol, 677 mg sodium

PREPARATION TIME: *10 min.*
COOKING TIME: *15 min.*

1/2 cup chicken broth
1 tsp. **each** sugar and vinegar
1 Tbsp. soy sauce
1/2 tsp. salt
Dash of pepper
1 large eggplant or
   3 Japanese eggplants
   (about 1 1/4 lb. total)
5 Tbsp. salad oil
1/4 lb. lean ground pork
2 green onions (including
   tops), finely chopped
1 tsp. minced fresh ginger
2 tsp. minced garlic
2 tsp. hot bean sauce, or 2
   small dried hot red chiles,
   crumbled, seeded
1 tsp. cornstarch and 1
   Tbsp. water, mixed
1 tsp. sesame oil

In a bowl, stir together broth, sugar, vinegar, soy sauce, salt, and pepper; set aside. Peel eggplant, if desired (don't peel Japanese eggplant); cut into strips 2 inches long and 1/2 inch thick.

Place a wok over medium-high heat. When wok is hot, add 3 tablespoons of the salad oil. When oil is hot, add eggplant and stir-fry for 3 minutes. (Eggplant will soak up oil immediately; stir constantly to prevent burning.) Remove from wok and set aside.

Pour remaining 2 tablespoons salad oil into wok. When oil is hot, crumble in pork and add onions, ginger, garlic, and bean sauce. Stir-fry until meat is no longer pink (about 2 minutes). Return eggplant to wok and pour in broth mixture; cover and cook over medium-low heat until eggplant is tender when pierced (about 6 minutes).

Stir cornstarch-water mixture; pour into wok and stir until sauce boils and thickens. Stir in sesame oil.

Makes 4 servings

Sesame-topped Vegetables

S T I R - F R Y

*Malaysian "achar", a colorful tumble of sweet-and-sour
vegetables, provides a cooling contrast to any spicy entrée.
Serve warm or at room temperature.*

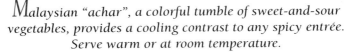

PER SERVING: *220 calories, 4 g protein, 20 g carbohydrates, 16 g total fat, 0 mg cholesterol, 25 mg sodium*

PREPARATION TIME: *10 min.*
COOKING TIME: *8 min.*

½ *English or European
  cucumber*
3 large carrots
3 cups cauliflowerets
½ *cup sesame seeds*
⅓ *cup salad oil*
*2 cloves garlic, minced
  or pressed*
½ *cup minced shallots*
½ *cup distilled white
  vinegar*
¼ *cup sugar*
Soy sauce
Arugula leaves (optional)

Cut cucumber and carrots into thin, about 6-inch-long slivers. Break cauliflowerets into smaller flowerets. Set vegetables aside.

Place a wok over medium heat. When wok is hot, add sesame seeds and stir until golden (2 to 3 minutes). Pour out of wok and set aside.

Pour oil into wok. When oil is hot, add garlic and shallots; stir-fry until shallots are soft. Increase heat to high and add vinegar, sugar, cauliflowerets, and carrots. Stir-fry until vegetables are tender-crisp to bite; add cucumber and stir-fry until hot. Season to taste with soy sauce. Transfer to a serving plate; sprinkle with sesame seeds. Garnish with arugula, if desired.

Makes 6 to 8 servings

Silver Thread Stirred Eggs

Thin, near-transparent bean threads, also sold as cellophane or shining noodles, add a bouncy lightness to scrambled eggs, meat, and vegetables.

∞

PER SERVING: 295 calories, 17 g protein, 18 g carbohydrates, 17 g total fat, 335 mg cholesterol, 979 mg sodium

PREPARATION TIME: *10 min.*
SOAKING TIME: *30 min.*

2 oz. dried bean threads
4 dried Oriental mushrooms
2 tsp. soy sauce
6 eggs
1/2 tsp. salt
1/8 tsp. white pepper
2 Tbsp. salad oil
1 clove garlic, minced
1/4 lb. cooked ham, cut into
   match-stick pieces
1 stalk celery, thinly sliced
1/4 cup sliced bamboo shoots
2 green onions (including
   tops), thinly sliced

Soak bean threads in warm water for 30 minutes, then drain and cut into 4-inch lengths. Also soak mushrooms in 3/4 cup warm water for 30 minutes. Remove mushrooms from water. Pour 1/2 cup of the soaking water into a bowl; stir in soy sauce. Cut off and discard mushroom stems; squeeze caps dry and thinly slice. Set mushrooms and bean threads aside.

In a bowl, beat eggs with salt and white pepper; set aside.

Place a wok over high heat; when wok is hot, add oil. When oil begins to heat, add garlic and stir once; then add ham and mushrooms and stir-fry for 1 minute. Add celery and bamboo shoots and stir-fry for 2 minutes. Add bean threads and mushroom water and cook until liquid is absorbed. Add onions and cook for 30 seconds. Reduce heat to medium. Pour eggs into wok; turn eggs occasionally with a spatula, until eggs are set but still soft and creamy.

Makes 4 servings

Chinese Ginger-Garlic Asparagus

*Crisp stir-fried asparagus is especially
tasty when accented with garlic and fresh ginger;
broccoli benefits from the same treatment.*

~

PER SERVING: 82 calories, 3 g protein, 4 g carbohydrates, 7 g total fat, 0 mg cholesterol, 2 mg sodium

PREPARATION TIME: *10 min.*
COOKING TIME: *5 min.*

1 lb. asparagus
2 Tbsp. salad oil
1 large clove garlic,
  minced or pressed
1/2 to 1 tsp. grated fresh
  ginger
2 Tbsp. water

Snap off and discard tough ends of the asparagus,
then cut asparagus spears into 1/4-inch slanting slices.

Place a wok over high heat; when the wok is hot,
add oil. When oil begins to heat, add the garlic and
fresh ginger and stir once; then add asparagus and
stir-fry for 1 minute.

Add water; cover and cook until asparagus is
tender-crisp to bite (2 to 3 minutes).

Makes 4 servings

Sweet & Sour
Carrots

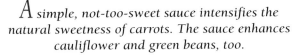

A simple, not-too-sweet sauce intensifies the natural sweetness of carrots. The sauce enhances cauliflower and green beans, too.

PER SERVING: 127 calories, 2 g protein, 23 g carbohydrates, 4 g total fat, 0 mg cholesterol, 151 mg sodium

PREPARATION TIME: *10 min.*
COOKING TIME: *8 min.*

1/4 cup chicken broth
2 Tbsp. **each** vinegar and
  firmly packed brown sugar
1 Tbsp. cornstarch
1 Tbsp. salad oil
1 lb. carrots (about 4
  medium-size), cut into 1/4-
  inch-thick slanting slices
1 small onion, cut in half,
  then cut crosswise into
  1/4-inch-thick slices
3 Tbsp. chicken broth
Salt
Minced parsley (optional)

In a bowl, stir together the 1/4 cup broth, vinegar, sugar, and cornstarch. Set aside.

Place a wok over high heat; when wok is hot, add oil. When oil is hot, add carrots and onion and stir-fry for 1 minute. Add the 3 tablespoons broth and reduce heat to medium; cover and cook until carrots are tender-crisp to bite. Increase heat to high. Stir cornstarch mixture, pour into wok, and stir until sauce boils and thickens. Season to taste with salt. Sprinkle with parsley, if desired.

Makes 4 servings

Green Beans with Garlic

*Those familiar Asian seasonings of soy sauce, sherry,
ginger, and garlic enhance just about any food; here, they accent
tender-crisp green beans. Sesame seeds add extra crunch.*

∞

PER SERVING: *106 calories, 3 g protein, 11 g carbohydrates, 6 g total fat, 0 mg cholesterol, 351 mg sodium*

PREPARATION TIME: *10 min.*
COOKING TIME: *15 min.*

*4 tsp. soy sauce
1 tsp. sugar
1 Tbsp. dry sherry or water
1 Tbsp. sesame seeds
1½ Tbsp. salad oil
3 cloves garlic, minced
  or pressed
1 Tbsp. minced fresh ginger
1 lb. green beans (ends
  removed), cut diagonally
  into 2-inch lengths*

In a small bowl, stir together soy sauce, sugar, and sherry; set aside.

Place a wok over medium heat; when wok is hot, add sesame seeds and stir until golden (about 2 minutes). Pour out of wok and set aside.

Increase heat to medium-high and pour oil into wok. When oil is hot, add garlic, ginger, and beans; stir-fry for 1½ minutes. Stir in soy sauce mixture; reduce heat to medium, cover, and cook until beans are tender-crisp to bite (4 to 7 minutes).

Uncover, increase heat to high, and boil, stirring, until almost all liquid has evaporated (1 to 3 minutes). Pour onto a warmed platter and sprinkle with sesame seeds.

Makes 4 servings

Parsnip & Carrot Sauté with Tarragon

A sprinkling of tarragon
is a perfect accent for sweet, tender carrots
and parsnips in this easy side dish.

PER SERVING: 221 calories, 2 g protein, 22 g carbohydrates, 15 g total fat, 39 mg cholesterol, 263 mg sodium

PREPARATION TIME: *10 min.*
COOKING TIME: *5 min.*

3 **each** medium-size
   parsnips and carrots
   (about 1¹/₂ lb. total)
5 Tbsp. butter or margarine
1 Tbsp. minced shallot
   or onion
¹/₃ cup chicken broth
1 Tbsp. fresh tarragon
   leaves, chopped, or 1¹/₂
   tsp. dry tarragon
2 Tbsp. minced parsley

Peel parsnips and carrots and cut into matchstick pieces. Set aside.

Place a wok over medium-high heat; when wok is hot, add butter. When butter is melted, add shallot and stir once. Add carrots and parsnips; stir-fry just until tender crisp to bite (about 2 minutes). Add broth, cover, and cook until tender to bite (2 to 3 more minutes). Stir in tarragon and parsley.

Makes 4 servings

MEAT & CHICKEN

Papaya & Sausage Sauté

Brought together in a spicy honey glaze, hearty bites of Italian sausage and smooth papaya slices make an exquisite entrée. When papayas aren't in season, try making the sauté with apples instead.

∞

PER SERVING: 499 calories, 22 g protein, 26 g carbohydrates, 35 g total fat, 88 mg cholesterol, 1012 mg sodium

PREPARATION TIME: *10 min.*
COOKING TIME: *12 min.*

1¹/₄ lb. mild Italian sausages, cut into ¹/₂-inch-thick slices
*2 Tbsp. **each** of lemon juice and honey*
*¹/₂ tsp. **each** ground ginger, ground coriander, and curry powder*
2 medium-size papayas (about 1 lb. each). peeled, seeded, cut lengthwise into ¹/₂-inch-thick slices
Green onions (roots and any wilted tops trimmed) and minced green onions tops (optional)

Place a wok over high heat; when wok is hot, add sausage. Stir-fry until browned (about 3 minutes). Discard all but 3 tablespoons of the drippings. Push sausage to side of work; stir lemon juice, honey, ginger, coriander, and curry powder into drippings at bottom of wok. Then push sausage into spice mixture and toss to coat; transfer to a serving plate and keep warm.

Add papayas to wok. Cook over high heat, turning occasionally, until fruit is glazed and light brown (3 to 5 minutes). Arrange papayas attractively around sausage. Garnish with whole and minced green onions, if desired.

Makes about 4 servings

Szechwan Beef

Hot chiles, characteristic of Szechwan province, boldly accent lean, tender strips of sirloin in this satisfying beef dish. Slender carrot ribbons and sliced bamboo shoots contribute color and crispness.

∽

PER SERVING: *330 calories, 27 g protein, 14 g carbohydrates, 19 g total fat, 69 mg cholesterol, 593 mg sodium*

PREPARATION TIME: *10 min.*
COOKING TIME: *10 min.*

2 Tbsp. soy sauce
1 Tbsp. dry sherry
2 tsp. sugar
½ tsp. cornstarch
1 lb. boneless beef steak
   (such as top round, flank,
   or sirloin)
2 Tbsp. salad oil
16 dried hot red chiles
2 large carrots, cut into
   3-inch-long julienne strips
1 can (about 8 oz.) sliced
   bamboo shoots, drained
   (and thinly sliced, if
   desired)
Fresh cilantro leaves
   (optional)

Mix together the soy sauce, sherry, sugar, and cornstarch; set aside. Cut beef with the grain into 1½-inch-wide strips; then cut each strip across the grain into ⅛-inch-thick slanting slices. Set aside.

Place a wok over high heat; when wok is hot, add oil. When oil is hot, add chiles and cook, stirring, until chiles just begin to char. Remove chiles from wok; set aside.

Add beef to wok and stir-fry until browned (1½ to 2 minutes); remove from wok and set aside. Add carrots to wok and stir-fry until tender-crisp to bite (about 3 minutes). Add bamboo shoots and stir-fry for 1 more minute.

Return meat and chiles to wok; stir soy sauce mixture and add to wok. Stir until sauce boils and thickens. Garnish with cilantro, if desired.

Makes 4 servings

Black Bean Spareribs

These ribs bear little resemblance to their Texan counterpart. You'll need to have the ribs cut for you; they're sawed through the bones into short strips, then cut apart between the bones.

꩜

PER SERVING: *471 calories, 27 g protein, 6 g carbohydrates, 37 g total fat, 108 mg cholesterol, 1082 mg sodium*

PREPARATION TIME: *15 min.*
MARINATING TIME: *15 min.*
COOKING TIME: *1 hr.*

*2 Tbsp. fermented salted
   black beans, rinsed,
   drained, finely chopped*
*2 cloves garlic, minced
   or pressed*
1 tsp. chopped fresh ginger
*1 Tbsp. **each** cornstarch,
   dry sherry, and soy sauce*
*1/2 tsp. **each** salt and sugar*
*1 1/2 lb. spareribs, cut 1 1/2
   inches long, then cut apart
   between bones*
2 Tbsp. salad oil
*Thinly sliced green
   onion tops*

In a bowl, stir together black beans, garlic, ginger, cornstarch, sherry, soy sauce, salt, and sugar. Add ribs and turn until well coated; let marinate for 15 minutes.

Place a wok over high heat; when wok is hot, add oil. When oil is hot, add meat and cook, turning once, until browned on both sides (about 4 minutes). Transfer to an 8- or 9-inch round heatproof bowl.

Rinse wok. Place bowl on a rack in wok over 1 1/2 to 2 inches of boiling water. Cover and steam until meat is tender when pierced (about 1 hour). Skim fat from sauce; sprinkle meat with onions.

Makes 2 or 3 servings

Fajitas Stir-fry

STIR-FRY

Fajitas in a wok? Yes—when you make this hearty stir-fried version of the Southwestern barbecue classic. Fun, delicious, and quick, Fajitas Stir-fry is sure to become a favorite.

∞

PER SERVING: *589 calories, 35 g protein, 56 g carbohydrates, 26 g total fat, 65 mg cholesterol, 412 mg sodium*

PREPARATION TIME: *30 min.*
COOKING TIME: *7 min.*

1 lb. lean boneless beef steak
1 large ripe avocado
2 Tbsp. salad oil
2 cloves garlic, minced or
  pressed
1 large onion, thinly sliced,
  separated into rings
2 or 3 fresh jalapeño chiles,
  seeded and minced
1 large red bell pepper,
  seeded, thinly sliced
2 tsp. ground cumin
3 Tbsp. lime juice
1 tsp. cornstarch
2 medium-size pear-shaped
  tomatoes, diced
Salt and pepper
Lime wedges
8 warm flour tortillas
Sour cream
Salsa (optional)

Cut beef with the grain into 1-inch-wide strips, then cut each strip across the grain into 1/8-inch-thick slices. Set aside. Pit, peel, and dice avocado.

Place a wok over high heat; when wok is hot, add 1 tablespoon of the oil. When oil is hot, add meat. Stir-fry until meat is browned (1½ to 2 minutes); transfer meat to a bowl with a slotted spoon.

Add remaining 1 tablespoon of oil to wok, then add garlic, onion, chiles, and bell pepper. Stir-fry until onion is soft (about 3 minutes). Stir together cumin, lime juice, and cornstarch; add to wok. Return meat to wok, add tomatoes, and stir until mixture is hot and juices boil. Season to taste with salt and pepper, then pour fajitas into a serving dish; garnish with lime wedges.

Spoon meat mixture onto tortilla; add sour cream, avocado, and a squeeze of lime to taste. Fold up and accompany with salsa.

Makes 4 servings

Hot Beef &
Watercress Salad

Start this main dish by stir-frying strips of marinated beef. Then spoon the sizzling meat over cool, crisp watercress and onions to create Hot Beef & Watercress Salad. Serve fresh tangerines for dessert.

⌒

PER SERVING: *260 calories, 30 g protein, 12 g carbohydrates, 11 g total fat, 65 mg cholesterol, 452 mg sodium*

PREPARATION TIME: *10 min.*
MARINATING TIME: *30 min.*
COOKING TIME: *3 min.*

*¹/₂ lb. lean boneless beef
   steak (such as top round,
   flank, or sirloin), cut about
   1 inch thick
4 cloves garlic, minced
   or pressed
2 tsp. soy sauce
1 tsp. sugar
1 Tbsp. salad oil
2 Tbsp. white wine vinegar
¹/₄ tsp. pepper
1 small white onion,
   thinly sliced, separated
   into rings
About ¹/₂ lb. watercress*

Cut beef with grain into 3-inch-wide strips, then cut each strip across the grain into ¹/₈-inch-thick slanting slices. In a bowl, stir together garlic, soy sauce, ¹/₂ teaspoon of the sugar, and 1 teaspoon of the oil. Add beef; stir to coat. Cover and refrigerate for at least 30 minutes or until next day.

In another bowl, stir together remaining ¹/₂ teaspoon sugar, remaining 2 teaspoons of oil, vinegar and pepper. Add onion and mix lightly. Cover and refrigerate for at least 30 minutes or until next day.

Remove and discard tough watercress stems; rinse sprigs thoroughly and pat dry. Then measure 3 cups sprigs, lightly packed. Shortly before serving, add watercress to onion mixture, mixing lightly to coat. Arrange on 2 dinner plates.

Place a wok over high heat. When wok is hot, add beef mixture and stir-fry until meat is browned (1¹/₂ to 2 minutes). Arrange meat evenly atop watercress salads, and serve immediately.

Makes 2 servings

Chinese Chicken &
Zucchini

*Colorful and typically Oriental, this classic stir-fry
of crisp vegetable chunks and spicy chicken is a welcome meal in
any season. Its ingredients are easy to find all year round.*

PER SERVING: *299 calories, 28 g protein, 11 g carbohydrates, 15 g total fat, 65 mg cholesterol, 678 mg sodium*

PREPARATION TIME: *20 min,*
SOAKING TIME: *30 min.*
MARINATING TIME: *15 min.*
COOKING TIME: *10 min*

*5 dried Oriental mushrooms
2 tsp. **each** soy sauce, corn-
    starch, dry sherry,
    and water
Dash of white pepper
1 clove garlic, minced
1/2 tsp. minced fresh ginger
2 tsp. fermented salted black
    beans, rinsed, drained,
    chopped
1 1/2 lb. chicken breasts,
    skinned, boned
3 1/2 Tbsp. salad oil
1/2 lb. zucchini
1/2 cup sliced bamboo shoots
1 red bell pepper, seeded,
    cut in 1-inch squares
Oyster Cooking Sauce
    (recipe on page 7)*

Soak mushrooms for 30 minutes in enough warm water to cover, then drain. Cut off and discard stems; squeeze caps dry, thinly slice, and set aside.

In a bowl, mix soy sauce, cornstarch, sherry, water, pepper, garlic, ginger, and beans. Cut chicken into bite-size pieces; add to marinade and stir to coat, then stir in 1 1/2 teaspoons of the oil. Let marinate for 15 minutes. Slice zucchini diagonally.

Place a wok over high heat. When pan is hot, add 2 tablespoons of oil. When oil is hot, add chicken mixture. Stir-fry until meat is no longer pink in center (about 3 minutes); cut to test. Remove from pan; set aside.

Pour 1 tablespoon oil into wok. When oil is hot, add vegetables. Stir-fry for 1 minute, then add 2 tablespoons water, cover, and cook until zucchini and bell pepper are tender-crisp (about 3 more minutes). Return chicken to pan. Stir Oyster Cooking Sauce, pour into wok, and stir until sauce thickens.

Makes 3 or 4 servings

Hot & Sour Chicken

Peppery-hot foods are favored in the Chinese province of Hunan—a preference reflected in this spicy dish. Season the sauce with purchased red pepper flakes, or use crushed whole dried chiles (remove the seeds for a milder flavor).

∽

PER SERVING: *263 calories, 19 g protein, 9 g carbohydrates, 16 g total fat, 43 mg cholesterol, 940 mg sodium*

PREPARATION TIME: *15 min.*
COOKING TIME: *10 min.*

2 tsp. **each** *cornstarch, and dry sherry*
¹/₄ tsp. **each** *salt and pepper*
1 lb. *chicken breasts, skinned, boned, cut into ³/₄-inch cubes*
3 to 4 Tbsp. *salad oil*
1 Tbsp. *minced garlic*
2 tsp. *minced fresh ginger*
1 Tbsp. *fermented black beans, rinsed, drained, patted dry*
1 *green bell pepper, seeded, cut into 1-inch squares*
1 *carrot, thinly sliced*
1 *can (about 8 oz.) sliced bamboo shoots, drained*
1 Tbsp. *water*
Red Pepper Cooking Sauce (recipe on page 7)

In a bowl, mix cornstarch, sherry, salt, and pepper. Add chicken and stir to coat, then stir in 1½ teaspoons of the oil and let stand for 15 minutes to marinate.

Place a wok over high heat; when wok is hot, add 2 tablespoons of the oil. When oil begins to heat, add garlic, ginger, and black beans. Stir once, then add chicken mixture; stir-fry for about 3 minutes until opaque. Remove chicken from pan.

Add 1 tablespoon more oil to pan; when hot add bell pepper, carrot, and bamboo shoots; stir-fry for 30 seconds. Add water and stir-fry for another 1½ minutes. Return chicken to pan. Stir Red Pepper Cooking Sauce, add to pan, and cook, stirring until sauce boils and thickens.

Makes 4 servings

Many-spice Chicken

Distinctive taste results from a blend of herbs and spices and anise-flavored liqueur. If you don't enjoy a licoricelike taste, use dry sherry; you'll end up with an equally good—though different—dish.

⌒

PER SERVING: *464 calories, 35 g protein, 9 g carbohydrates, 29 g total fat, 86 mg cholesterol, 544 mg sodium*

PREPARATION TIME: *10 min.*
COOKING TIME: *5 min.*

1/4 cup salad oil
2 Tbsp. anise-flavored
liqueur or dry sherry
2 Tbsp. minced fresh ginger
1 tsp. **each** minced garlic
and soy sauce
3 Tbsp. thinly sliced green
onions (including tops)
1/4 tsp. **each** dry mustard,
chili powder, pepper, dry
oregano, dry sage, dry
thyme, ground cloves, and
ground cinnamon
1/4 tsp. **each** salt, sugar,
and all-purpose flour
1 whole chicken breast
(about 1 lb.), skinned,
boned, cut into bite-size
pieces
Chopped parsley

In a small bowl, stir 2 tablespoons of the oil together with liqueur, ginger, garlic, soy sauce, onions, mustard, chili powder, pepper, oregano, sage, thyme, cloves, cinnamon, salt, sugar, and flour. Set aside.

Place a wok over high heat; when wok is hot, add remaining 2 tablespoons oil. When oil is hot, add chicken and stir-fry until meat is no longer pink in center (about 3 minutes); cut to test. Add liqueur mixture and stir constantly until mixture boils and thickens (about 1 minute). Sprinkle with parsley.

Makes 2 servings

Stir-fried Chicken with Cheese

Tangy blue cheese lends creaminess and unusual flavor to this entrée. Season with wasabi paste, if you like, but watch out—it's hot. (You'll find it in Asian markets and well-stocked supermarkets.)

⌒⌒

PER SERVING: *776 calories, 55 g protein, 23 g carbohydrates, 54 g total fat, 168 mg cholesterol, 750 mg sodium*

PREPARATION TIME: *20 min.*
COOKING TIME: *15 min.*

1 lb. chicken thighs
 (about 3), skinned
2½ Tbsp. salad oil
½ cup raw shelled peanuts
 or unsalted dry-roasted
 peanuts
1 medium-size onion,
 thinly sliced
1 medium-size red bell
 pepper, seeded, cut
 into thin strips
2 cups bean sprouts
½ to 1 cup (2 to 4 oz.)
 coarsely crumbled blue-
 veined cheese
Soy sauce
Wasabi paste (optional)

Rinse chicken and pat dry. On inside of each thigh, cut meat to bone along entire length. With knife blade, scrape meat free from bone; then cut meat into 1-inch chunks.

Place a wok or 12-inch frying pan over medium-high heat. When wok is hot, add ½ tablespoon of the oil. When oil begins to heat, add peanuts; cook, stirring, until lightly toasted. Lift out and set aside.

Add the remaining 2 tablespoons of oil to the pan. When oil is hot, add chicken; cook, stirring, until no longer pink when slashed (3 to 5 minutes). Lift out and set aside.

Add onion and bell pepper to pan and cook, stirring, until onion is tender-crisp to bite (about 2 minutes). Add bean sprouts, peanuts, and chicken; stir until heated through.

Pour chicken mixture into a serving dish and gently mix in cheese. At the table, offer soy sauce and wasabi paste (if desired).

Makes about 2 servings

Thai Chicken &
Basil Stir-fry

For this exotic recipe, you'll find dried shiitakes, as well as the fish sauce and coconut milk you need for the cooking sauce, in Asian grocery stores and some supermarkets.

PER SERVING: *426 calories, 39 g protein, 20 g carbohydrates, 22 g total fat, 86 mg cholesterol, 882 mg sodium*

PREPARATION TIME: *25 min.*
COOKING TIME: *20 min.*

6 dried shiitake mushrooms (each 2 to 3 inches in diameter)
2 to 4 Tbsp salad oil
1 medium-size yellow onion, thinly sliced, separated into rings
3 cloves garlic, minced or pressed
2 Tbsp. minced fresh ginger
2 whole chicken breasts (about 1 lb. each), skinned, boned, cut into 1/2-inch-wide strips
Coconut Milk Cooking Sauce (recipe on page 7)
5 green onions (including tops), cut into 1-inch pieces
1 1/2 cups lightly packed slivered fresh basil leaves
Hot cooked rice

Soak mushrooms in warm water to cover until soft (10 to 15 minutes); drain well. Cut off and discard mushroom stems. Slice caps into 1/4-inch slivers; set aside.

Heat 2 tablespoons of the oil in a wok or large frying pan over high heat. Add yellow onion, garlic, and ginger; cook, stirring, until onion is lightly browned. With a slotted spoon, transfer onion mixture to a bowl; set aside. Add chicken to pan, a portion at a time (do not crowd pan); cook, stirring, until lightly browned (about 3 minutes) adding more oil as needed. As the chicken is cooked, lift out and add to onion mixture.

Pour Coconut Milk Cooking Sauce into pan; boil, stirring constantly, until reduced by about a third. Return onion mixture and chicken to pan. Add mushrooms, green onions, and basil; stir just until heated through. Serve over rice.

Makes 4 servings

SAVORY SEAFOOD

Shrimp Fried Rice

*F*ried rice provides an easy way to convert bits of leftovers into a one-dish meal. The embellishments are flexible; the rule for rice is not—you must start with cold, cooked rice so the grains remain separate when stir-fried.

⌒

PER SERVING: *420 calories, 15 g protein, 45 g carbohydrates, 20 g total fat, 140 mg cholesterol, 849 mg sodium*

PREPARATION TIME: *10 min.*
COOKING TIME: *8 min.*

4 cups cold, cooked
  long-grain rice
  (1¹/4 cups uncooked rice)
2 eggs
¹/4 tsp. salt
4 Tbsp. salad oil
2 whole green onions,
  thinly sliced
1 cup small cooked shrimp
  or diced cooked ham
  or chicken
¹/2 cup frozen peas, thawed
¹/2 cup roasted cashew nuts
2 Tbsp. soy sauce
¹/2 tsp. salt

Rub cooked rice with wet hands so all the grains are separated. Beat eggs with the ¹/4 teaspoon salt. In a wok, heat 1 tablespoon of the oil over medium heat. Add green onion and stir-fry for about 30 seconds. Add eggs and stir and cook until soft curds form; remove from pan and set aside.

Heat another tablespoon oil in pan. Add shrimp, peas, and cashews. Stir-fry for 2 minutes to heat through; remove from pan and set aside. Heat the remaining 2 tablespoons oil in pan. Add rice and stir-fry for 2 minutes to heat through. Stir in soy sauce and shrimp mixture. Add eggs and fold in until they are in small pieces. Season with salt.

Makes 4 or 5 servings

Chilled Salmon with Lomi Lomi Relish

Classic lomi lomi is a combination of chopped salted salmon, tomatoes, and onions. In this variation, though, the salmon is steamed and chilled separately, then served with an all-vegetable lomi lomi relish.

∞

PER SERVING: *289 calories, 37 g protein, 7 g carbohydrate, 12 g total fat, 100 mg cholesterol, 554 mg sodium*

PREPARATION TIME: *15 min.*
COOKING TIME: *6 to 10 min.*
CHILLING TIME: *30 min.*

*2 medium-size
  tomatoes, chopped*
*1 large green bell pepper,
  seeded, chopped*
*1/2 cup thinly sliced green
  onions, including tops*
1 small onion, chopped
*2 to 3 Tbsp. canned
  diced green chiles*
2 Tbsp. lemon juice
1 tsp. salt
*2 lb. salmon or turbot
  fillets, 3/4 to 1 inch thick*
2 bay leaves
Whole black peppercorns
Lemons
Butter lettuce leaves

Prepare Lomi Lomi Relish by combining first 7 ingredients; cover and refrigerate.

Place fish on a double layer of cheesecloth (slightly bigger all around than fish). Place bay leaves, peppercorns, and 4 lemon slices on fish. Then place fish on a rack in a wok over 1½ to 2 inches of boiling water, folding cheesecloth up around edges. Cover and steam until the fish flakes when prodded in thickest part (6 to 10 minutes). Grasp cheesecloth and lift out fish; cool. Discard seasonings, then cover and refrigerate fish until cold (30 minutes to 1 hour).

Arrange lettuce on 4 individual plates and top with serving-size pieces of fish. Serve with relish and lemon wedges.

*Makes 4 salmon servings,
2 cups relish*

Sweet & Sour Fish

Sweet-sour sauce is just as good with fish as it is with pork or chicken. Here, the familiar red sauce enhances a combination of bell pepper squares, tomato, and chunks of turbot or halibut.

⌒

PER SERVING: *746 calories, 35 g protein, 34 g carbohydrates, 52 g total fat, 104 mg cholesterol, 914 mg sodium*

PREPARATION TIME: *15 min.*
COOKING TIME: *12 min.*

1 Tbsp. cornstarch
1/4 cup sugar
*2 Tbsp. **each** soy sauce*
and catsup
1/4 cup distilled white vinegar
1/2 cup chicken broth
1/3 cup cornstarch
2 lb. turbot or halibut
fillets, cut into 1/2-inch
squares
6 Tbsp. salad oil
1 clove garlic, minced
1 onion, cut into 1-inch cubes
1 medium-size green bell
pepper, seeded, cut into
1/2-inch thick strips
1 medium-size tomato,
cut into 1-inch cubes
Fresh cilantro or Italian
parsley (optional)

Stir together 1 tablespoon cornstarch, sugar, soy sauce, catsup, vinegar, and chicken broth; set aside.

Place 1/3 cup cornstarch in a bag, add fish pieces, and shake to coat completely; shake off excess.

Place a wok over medium-high heat; when wok is hot, add 2 tablespoons of the oil. When oil is hot, add some of the fish; stir-fry until fish is browned on all sides and flakes when prodded (about 2 minutes). Remove from wok and keep warm. Repeat to cook remaining fish, adding about 2 tablespoons more oil.

Increase heat to high and pour 2 tablespoons more oil into wok. When oil is hot, add garlic, onion, and bell pepper; stir-fry for 2 minutes. Stir Sweet-Sour Sauce; pour into wok and stir in tomato. Bring to a boil, stirring. Return fish and any accumulated juices to wok; stir to combine. Garnish with cilantro, if desired.

Makes 4 servings

Crab Curry

This mild Cantonese curry of crab and vegetables is appealing to the eye and fun to eat, too. Finger food can be messy, though, so pass a basket of damp cloths around the table at the end of the meal.

⌒

PER SERVING: *266 calories, 21 g protein, 11 g carbohydrates, 15 g total fat, 112 mg cholesterol, 1234 mg sodium*

PREPARATION TIME: *15 min.*
COOKING TIME: *10 min.*

¾ cup chicken broth
*1 Tbsp. **each** cornstarch,*
  soy sauce, and dry sherry
*1 tsp. **each** salt and sugar*
4 tsp. curry powder
¼ lb. lean boneless pork
  (such as shoulder or butt),
  trimmed of excess fat,
  finely chopped or ground
1 large crab in shell
  (1½ to 2 lb.), cooked,
  cleaned, cracked
3 Tbsp. salad oil
1 large clove garlic, minced
1 medium-size onion,
  cut into wedges, layers
  separated
1 medium-size green bell
  pepper, seeded, cut
  into 1-inch squares
1 egg, lightly beaten

Stir together broth, cornstarch and sherry to make a cooking sauce, and set aside. Sprinkle salt, sugar, and curry powder over pork; mix well and set aside. Cut crab body into quarters; leave legs and claws whole. Set crab aside.

Place a wok over high heat. When wok is hot, add oil. When oil begins to heat, add garlic and stir once; then add seasoned pork and stir-fry until no longer pink (about 2 minutes). Add onion and bell pepper and stir-fry for 1 minute. Add crab and stir often until heated through (about 3 minutes). Stir cooking sauce, pour into wok, and stir until sauce boils and thickens. Add egg, stir just until egg begins to set (about 30 seconds).

Makes 3 or 4 servings

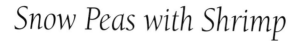

Snow Peas with Shrimp

For a meal in minutes, try this snappy stir-fry of shrimp, water chestnuts, and sweet snow peas. If you like, leave the tails on the shrimp for an attractive presentation.

⊂⊃

PER SERVING: *265 calories, 22 g protein, 15 g carbohydrates, 12 g total fat, 140 mg cholesterol, 783 mg sodium*

PREPARATION TIME: *20 min.*
COOKING TIME: *5 min.*

1 tsp. cornstarch
1/4 tsp. ground ginger
2 Tbsp. **each** soy sauce
    and dry sherry
1/2 cup chicken broth
3 Tbsp. salad oil
1 clove garlic, minced
    or pressed
1 lb. medium-size raw
    shrimp, shelled, deveined
1 1/2 cups snow peas
    or sugar snap peas,
    ends, strings removed
1 can (8 oz.) water
    chestnuts, drained,
    thinly sliced
2 or 3 green onions
    (including tops),
    thinly sliced

Stir together cornstarch, ground ginger, soy sauce, sherry, and chicken broth to make a cooking sauce, and set aside while preparing other ingredients.

Place a wok over high heat; when wok is hot, add oil. When oil is hot, add garlic and shrimp and stir-fry for about 1 minute. Add snow peas and stir-fry for about 3 minutes. Add water chestnuts and onions; stir until mixed.

Stir cooking sauce and add to ingredients in wok; stir until sauce boils and thickens and shrimp turn pink. Serve immediately.

Makes 4 servings

Stir-fried Shrimp with
Peking Sauce

*Light eating is a virtue and a pleasure when the meal includes
Stir-Fried Shrimp with Peking Sauce. These tender shrimp are tossed with
a colorful mélange of vegetables and served with fluffy white rice.*

∽

PER SERVING: *256 calories, 23 g protein, 22 g carbohydrates, 9 g total fat, 140 mg cholesterol, 1184 mg sodium*

PREPARATION TIME: *30 min.*
COOKING TIME: *6 to 8 min.*

*2 cloves garlic, minced
    or pressed
2 Tbsp. minced fresh ginger
    or 1 tsp. ground ginger
¹/₂ cup water
¹/₄ cup hoisin sauce
2 Tbsp. soy sauce
1 Tbsp. rice vinegar
2 tsp. sugar
2 Tbsp. salad oil
1 lb. medium-size shrimp,
    shelled, deveined
1 large red onion, slivered
2 cups broccoli flowerets
1 **each** red and yellow or
    green bell peppers, seeded,
    cut into long strips
2 to 4 Tbsp. water
2 tsp. cornstarch*

Stir together garlic, ginger, ¹/₂ cup water, hoisin
sauce, soy sauce, rice vinegar, and sugar to make
a Peking Stir-fry Cooking Sauce; set aside.

Place a wok or wide nonstick frying pan over
high heat. When pan is hot, add 1 tablespoon of the
oil, then shrimp. Stir-fry just until shrimp are pink
(about 2 minutes). Remove shrimp from pan. Then
add to pan remaining oil, onion, broccoli, bell pep-
pers, and 1 tablespoon of the water. Stir-fry, adding
water as needed, until broccoli is barely tender to
bite (2 to 4 minutes).

Blend cornstarch into prepared cooking sauce.
Add mixture to pan and stir just until sauce is
thickened and clear. Add shrimp, stirring just until
heated through. Serve immediately.

Makes 4 servings

Lemony Fish with Asparagus

*Bright green asparagus and delicate
white-fleshed fish are flavored with fresh lemon
in this simple and elegant entrée.*

⌒

PER SERVING: 240 calories, 15 g protein, 4 g carbohydrates, 19 g total fat, 17 mg cholesterol, 88 mg sodium

PREPARATION TIME: *10 min.*
COOKING TIME. *5 min.*

1 lb. asparagus spears
2 tsp. **each** cornstarch,
    lemon juice, and salad oil
3/4 lb. orange roughy,
    sea bass, or halibut fillets,
    each about 1/2 inch thick,
    cut into 1- by 3-inch strips
3 Tbsp. salad oil
1 large clove garlic,
    minced or pressed
2 Tbsp. chicken broth
    or water
2 Tbsp. lemon juice

Snap off and discard tough ends of asparagus;
cut spears into 1/2 inch slanting slices. Set aside.

In a bowl, stir together cornstarch, the 2 teaspoons lemon juice, and the 2 teaspoons oil.
Add fish and stir gently until evenly coated.

Place a wok over medium-high heat; when wok
is hot, add 2 tablespoons of the oil. When oil is hot,
add fish and stir-fry until opaque (about 2 minutes);
remove fish from wok and set aside.

Pour remaining 1 tablespoon oil into wok.
When oil begins to heat, add garlic; stir-fry for about
30 seconds. Then add asparagus and stir-fry for
1 minute. Stir together broth and the 2 tablespoons
lemon juice; pour into wok, cover, and cook, stirring
often, until asparagus is tender-crisp to bite (2 or 3
more minutes). Return fish and any accumulated
juices to wok and stir just until heated through.

Makes 3 or 4 servings

Sautéed Oysters with Basil

Made with just five ingredients, this dish could hardly be simpler or quicker. You just brown oysters in butter with a little chopped basil, then make a speedy sauce by stirring white wine into the pan juices.

PER SERVING: 219 calories, 9 g protein, 11 g carbohydrates, 14 g total fat, 93 mg cholesterol, 245 mg sodium

PREPARATION TIME: *10 min.*
COOKING TIME: *5 min.*

1/2 lb. shucked fresh
 oysters, drained
All-purpose flour
2 Tbsp. butter or margarine
1 Tbsp. chopped fresh basil
 or 1/2 tsp. dry basil
2 Tbsp. dry white wine

Cut any large oysters into bite-size pieces. Pat oysters dry on paper towels; dredge in flour and shake off excess. Place a wok over medium-high heat; when wok is hot, add butter. When butter is melted, add oysters and sprinkle with basil. Stir-fry until oysters are golden brown (about 3 minutes), then transfer to a serving dish.

Add wine to wok and cook until sauce is reduced to 1 tablespoon. Spoon sauce over oysters.

Makes 2 servings

Shrimp &
Vegetable Salad

Crisp vegetables and small shrimp are chilled
in a soy-flavored marinade and topped with crunchy cashews
to make a satisfying one-dish lunch.

∞

PER SERVING: *210 calories, 14 g protein, 14 g carbohydrates, 12 g total fat, 55 mg cholesterol, 638 mg sodium*

PREPARATION TIME: *20 min.*
COOKING TIME: *6 min.*
CHILLING TIME: *4 hrs.*

½ lb. broccoli
2 Tbsp. salad oil
2 cloves garlic, minced
¾ tsp. minced fresh ginger
½ lb. mushrooms,
   thinly sliced
½ lb. snow peas, ends
   and strings removed
Oyster Cooking Sauce
   (recipe on page 7)
1 can (4½ oz.) small
   shrimp, drained
½ cup mayonnaise (optional)
Salad greens, such as butter
   lettuce leaves, endive
   spears, dandelion greens
¼ cup salted roasted cashews
   or slivered almonds
1 jar (2 oz.) sliced pimentos,
   drained

Cut off and discard tough ends of broccoli stalks. Cut flowerets off stalks; then cut flowerets into ¼-inch-thick slices. Peel stalks and cut crosswise into ⅛-inch-thick slices. Set aside.

Place a wok over high heat; when wok is hot, add oil. When oil begins to heat, add garlic and ginger and stir-fry for 1 minute. Add broccoli, mushrooms, and snow peas; stir-fry just until broccoli and peas are tender-crisp to bite (3 to 4 minutes). Pour into a bowl.

Prepare Oyster Cooking Sauce. Pour sauce over vegetables; then stir in shrimp. Let cool, then cover and refrigerate for at least 4 hours. Drain vegetable mixture, discarding liquid. If desired, stir in mayonnaise. Spoon over salad greens, sprinkle with cashews, and garnish with pimentos.

Makes 4 servings

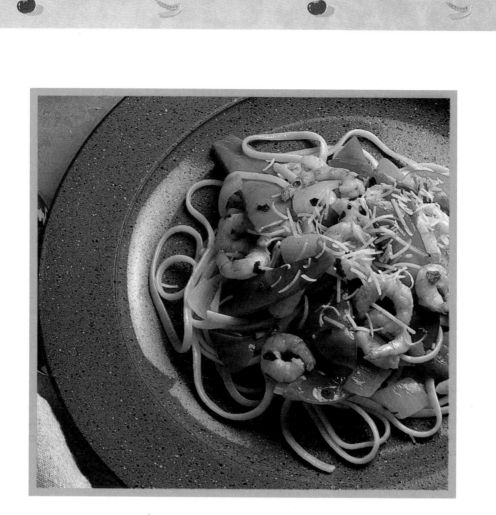

Italian Stir-fried Pasta

*D*inner *can be on the table in under half an hour when you serve this dish of al dente pasta mixed with onion, bell pepper, and small shrimp and topped with plenty of Parmesan cheese.*

᳁

PER SERVING: *792 calories, 57 g protein, 74 g carbohydrates, 29 g total fat, 363 mg cholesterol, 1113 mg sodium*

PREPARATION TIME: *10 min.*
COOKING TIME: *15 min.*

6 oz. dried linguine or
  other thin pasta
Boiling salted water
2 Tbsp. olive oil
1 small onion, cut into
  bite-size pieces
1 medium-size green bell
  pepper, seeded, cut
  into bite-size pieces
¼ to ½ tsp. crushed
  dried hot red chiles
½ to 1 tsp. dried oregano
1 Tbsp. butter or margarine
2 oz. (about 18) snow peas,
  ends and strings removed
¾ lb. small cooked,
  shelled shrimp
About ½ cup grated
  Parmesan cheese

Following package directions, cook linguine in boiling salted water until barely al dente; drain well and pour onto a hot platter.

While pasta is cooking, place a wok over high heat; when wok is hot, add oil. When oil is hot, add onion, bell pepper, chiles, and oregano. Stir-fry until vegetables are tender to bite (about 5 minutes).

Reduce heat to medium-high. Add butter to wok; when butter is melted, add snow peas and stir-fry for 1 minute. Add shrimp, stir well, and remove wok from heat.

Spoon hot stir-fried mixture over drained pasta and serve at once. Offer cheese to sprinkle on individual servings.

Makes 2 servings

Index